The Bethune Blueprint
Transforming Your Life Using the Lessons of
Dr. Mary McLeod Bethune

Companion Workbook

Writen By & Designed By

Dr. Evelyn Bethune

TABLE OF CONTENTS

Chapter 1 — 8---13
Build Your House on a Solid Foundation

Chapter 2 — 14----21
Courageous Convictions: Channeling Inner Strength

Chapter 3 — 22----27
Empowering Education: Elevating Through Knowledge

Chapter 4 — 28----32
Resilient Resonance: Rising Above Strife

Chapter 5 — 33----36
Sisterhood and Solidarity: Building Supportive Networks

Chapter 6 — 37----41
Political Prowess: Advocating for Equality

Chapter 7 — 42----45
Trailblazing Tenets: Defining Your Path

Chapter 8 — 46----50
Radiant Resurgence: Reclaiming Your Power

Chapter 9 — 51----54
Visionary Vibrance: Imagining a Brighter Future

Chapter 10 — 55----60
Mastering Mindfulness: Cultivating Inner Peace

Chapter 11 — 61----65
Bountiful Blessings: Cultivating Gratitude and Generosity

Chapter 12 — 66----69
Legacy of Love: Embodying the Spirit of Dr. Mary McLeod Bethune

CHAPTER 1

BUILD YOUR HOUSE ON A SOLID FOUNDATION

Daily Worksheet:
Embracing Your Legacy

Date: _____

Today's Affirmation: "I am capable of extraordinary things. My roots, resilience, and vision drive my growth and the upliftment of my community."

1. Embrace Your Roots:

Today, I am grateful for...

(i)_____
_____
_____

(ii)_____
_____
_____

(iii)_____
_____

2. Prioritize Education:

Today's learning goal:

_____
_____

New thing I learned today:

_____
_____

3. Stay Resilient:

Challenges I encountered today:

_____
_____
_____

How I overcame these challenges:

(i)_____
_____
_____

(ii)_____
_____
_____

(iii)_____
_____
_____

4. Unite and Empower:

Today, I have contributed to my community by:

_____
_____
_____

One new way I can empower someone in my community tomorrow:

_____
_____
_____

5. Be Visionary:

My long-term vision:

_____
_____
_____

Small steps I took today to realize this vision:

(i)_____
_____
_____

(ii)_____
_____
_____

(iii)_____
_____
_____

6. Reflections:

Highlights of my day:

(i)_____

_____

_____

(ii)_____

_____

_____

(iii)_____

_____

_____

How I felt today (rate from 1-10, with 1 being low and 10 high): _____

What I can do tomorrow to make my day better:

_____

_____

_____

Use this worksheet daily as a guide to connect with your roots, prioritize education, maintain resilience, unite and empower your community, and be visionary - just as **Dr. Mary McLeod Bethune** did. Remember, every day is a step towards discovering your authentic self and achieving greatness.

7 Affirmations

1. "Just as Dr. Bethune rose above challenges, I am equipped and destined to overcome any obstacles in my path to greatness."

2. "My roots, heritage, and the trailblazers before me empower my journey towards success and fulfillment."

3. "Every day, I commit to lifelong learning and growth, understanding that knowledge is the key to unlocking my potential."

4. "I am resilient, drawing strength from adversity, and using challenges as stepping stones towards my purpose."

5. "Inspired by Dr. Bethune, I lead with grace, determination, and vision, impacting those around me positively."

6. "I harness my influence to advocate for positive change, ensuring that my voice creates ripples of transformation in my community and beyond."

7. "Empowered by the lessons of Dr. Mary McLeod Bethune, I am on a journey of self-discovery, purpose, and greatness."

CHAPTER 2

COURAGEOUS CONVICTIONS:
CHANNELING INNER STRENGTH

Daily Worksheet:

Discovering Your Authentic Self and Purpose Inspired by Black Icons

Date: _____

1. Define Your Mission

_____
_____
_____

Reflect on your passions and the causes you deeply care about.
What change do you aspire to create in your community?
Take inspiration from your favorite Black icons.

_____
_____
_____

Today's mission: [Fill in]

_____
_____
_____

How does it align with the vision of a Black icon you admire: [Fill in]

_____
_____
_____

2. Cultivate Courage

_____
_____
_____

Identify a fear or doubt that's holding you back. Now, think of a

_____

_____

_____

A Black icon who overcame a similar fear or challenge. What steps did they take? How can you apply their strategies in your life?

_____

_____

_____

Fear/Doubt to Overcome Today: [Fill in]

_____

_____

_____

Black Icon for Inspiration: [Fill in]

_____

_____

_____

Action Steps to Overcome this Fear/Doubt: [Fill in]

_____

_____

_____

3. Uphold Your Commitments

_____
_____
_____

A Black icon who overcame a similar fear or challenge. What steps did they take? How can you apply their strategies in your life?

_____
_____
_____

Commitment for Today: [Fill in]

_____
_____
_____

Black Icon for Inspiration: [Fill in]

_____
_____
_____

Action Step to Uphold this Commitment: [Fill in]

_____
_____
_____

4. Nurture Your Tenacity

_____
_____
_____

Identify a challenge or setback you're currently facing. Choose a Black icon who demonstrated resilience in the face of adversity. What can you learn from their experience?

_____
_____
_____

Current Challenge/Setback: [Fill in]

_____
_____
_____

Black Icon for Inspiration: [Fill in]

_____
_____
_____

Action Step to Cultivate Resilience: [Fill in]

_____
_____
_____

5. Reflect on Your Progress

_____
_____
_____

Take some time to acknowledge your achievements and growth. Reflect on the lessons you've learned from the actions and lives of Black icons.

_____
_____
_____

Today's Achievements: [Fill in]

_____
_____
_____

Lessons Learned from Black Icons: [Fill in]

_____
_____
_____

6. Plan for Tomorrow

_____

_____

_____

Based on today's reflections and progress, set your intentions for the next day.

_____

_____

_____

Mission for Tomorrow: [Fill in]

_____

_____

_____

Fear/Doubt to Overcome: [Fill in]

_____

_____

_____

Commitment to Uphold: [Fill in]

_____

_____

_____

Challenge to Face with Resilience: [Fill in]

_____

_____

Daily Affirmation

Write a personal affirmation inspired by a quote from a Black icon, reminding you of your strength, purpose, and the value you bring to your community.

_____
_____
_____

Today's Affirmation: [Fill in]

_____
_____
_____

Black Icon Quote for Inspiration: [Fill in]

_____
_____
_____

Remember, this journey is about progress, not perfection. Each step you take brings you closer to realizing your purpose and the authentic self you are discovering. Be gentle with yourself and celebrate your accomplishments along the way.

CHAPTER 3

EMPOWERING EDUCATION:
ELEVATING THROUGH KNOWLEDGE

Daily Worksheet:

Date: _____

1. Embrace Lifelong Learning:

Today's learning goal:

_____
_____
_____

Resource(s) to use (book, course, workshop, etc.):

_____
_____
_____

Time spent on learning:

_____
_____
_____

2. Share Your Knowledge and Experiences:

Who can you mentor or support today?

_____
_____

What knowledge or experience can you share with them?

_____
_____
_____

How did you share your knowledge or experience? (conversation, email, social media post, etc.)

_____
_____
_____

3. Cultivate Curiosity and Encourage Learning in Others:

Who can you encourage to learn today?

_____
_____
_____

How will you encourage their learning? (Suggest a resource, ask an open-ended question, etc.)

_____
_____
_____

Result of your encouragement:

_____
_____
_____

4. Advocate for Change and Raise Awareness About Important Issues:

The issue you are passionate about:

_____
_____
_____

The action you will take to advocate or raise awareness today:

_____
_____
_____

Outcome or progress made as a result of your action:

_____
_____
_____

5. Build Supportive Networks and Connections:

New connection(s) or collaboration(s) to pursue today:

_____
_____
_____

How will you connect or collaborate with them? (email, phone call, in-person meeting, etc.)

_____
_____
_____

Outcome or progress made as a result of your connection or collaboration:

_____
_____
_____

Reflection:

What did you learn today, and how can you apply it to your life?

_____
_____
_____

How did you contribute to the growth and empowerment of yourself and others today?

_____
_____
_____

What can you do tomorrow to continue building on today's progress?

_____
_____

7 Affirmations

1. I am a lifelong learner, constantly growing and evolving on my journey to greatness.

2. My experiences and knowledge hold immense value, and I am eager to share them with others.

3. I am an advocate for change, using my voice and actions to make a positive impact on the world around me.

4. I embrace curiosity and encourage those around me to learn and expand their horizons.

5. I am dedicated to building supportive networks, and fostering connections that empower myself and others.

6. I am inspired by the resilience and determination of trailblazing Black women who have come before me.

7. I am walking in the footsteps of Dr. Mary McLeod Bethune, honoring her legacy by living a life of purpose and greatness.

CHAPTER 4

RESILIENT RESONANCE: RISING ABOVE STRIFE

Daily Worksheet: Unleashing your Resilient Resonance

Date: _____

Morning Reflections

My affirmation for the day is:

_____
_____
_____

Today, I will be brave by:

_____
_____
_____

My intention for today to cultivate my inner fortitude is:

_____
_____
_____

Action Steps

Action Step 1: Recognizing barriers

Today's barrier I will bravely confront:

_____
_____
_____

Plan to overcome:

_____

_____

_____

Action Step 2: Cultivating fortitude

The way I will foster my steadfast spirit today is:

_____

_____

_____

Reflection on the process:

_____

_____

_____

Action Step 3: Connecting with others

The person I will connect with today for shared growth:

_____

_____

_____

How I intend to engage:

_____

_____

Action Step 4: Mobilizing for change

How I intend to spark a unified uprising and foster positive change today:

_____
_____
_____

Reflection on the process:

_____
_____
_____

Evening Reflections

Today, I felt brave when:

_____
_____
_____

A moment where I felt my steadfast spirit was:

_____
_____
_____

A moment where I felt connected with others was:

_____
_____
_____

How I mobilized for change today:

_____
_____
_____

My affirmation for tomorrow is:

_____
_____
_____

Signature: _____

CHAPTER 5

SISTERHOOD AND SOLIDARITY:
BUILDING SUPPORTIVE NETWORKS

Daily Empowerment Worksheet

Date: _____

Step 1: Educate Yourself

Today's topic: _____

Key points learned: _____

How will you apply this knowledge to your daily life or goals?

_____

_____

_____

Step 2: Join the NCNW or a Similar Organization

Organization: _____

Today's activities or events: _____

What did you learn or gain from participating? _____

Step 3: Engage in Mentorship

Mentor or Mentee: _____

Today's discussion topic or goal: _____

Key takeaways or insights: _____

Step 4: Get Involved in Your Community

Local organization or initiative: _____

Today's activities or events: _____

What impact did your involvement have? _____

Step 5: Advocate for Change

Issue or cause: _____

Today's advocacy actions (e.g., social media posts, conversations, contacting representatives): _____
_____

Outcome or progress made: _____

Reflection:

Today's successes:

_____
_____
_____

Areas for improvement:

_____
_____
_____

Goals for tomorrow:

_____
_____
_____

7 Affirmations that relate to this chapter

1. I am a powerful and influential force for change in my community, just like Dr. Mary McLeod Bethune.

2. I embrace the opportunity to learn from strong, intelligent women and to uplift others in return.

3. By connecting with like-minded individuals, I can make an even greater impact in the fight for equality and justice.

4. My faith in God and my unwavering determination propel me forward in my pursuit of empowering others.

5. I am committed to being a mentor and a mentee, nurturing growth and wisdom within myself and others.

6. As an advocate for change, I am actively using my voice and actions to create a more equitable and just world.

7. Every day, I choose to invest my time and energy in organizations and causes that align with my values and passions.

CHAPTER 6

POLITICAL PROWESS: ADVOCATING FOR EQUALITY

The Bethune Blueprint:
Daily Worksheet

Date: _____

Advocate for educational opportunities:

1. Today, I will support educational opportunities for all by:

Researching local initiatives and organizations that promote educational equity:

_____

_____

_____

Taking one action to support these initiatives or organizations (e.g., donate, volunteer, share on social media):

_____

_____

_____

Encourage mentorship and intergenerational connections:

2. Today, I will foster connections between different generations by:

Reaching out to a mentor or mentee to offer support or guidance:

_____

_____

_____

Attending or organizing an event that encourages intergenerational dialogue:

_____

_____

Promote representation and inclusivity:

3. Today, I will advocate for diverse voices and perspectives by:

Supporting or highlighting the work of a Black woman or another underrepresented individual in my field or community:

_____

_____

_____

Participating in or organizing a discussion, workshop, or event that promotes inclusivity and representation:

_____

_____

_____

Foster a spirit of resilience and determination:

4. Today, I will cultivate a resilient mindset by:

Reflecting on a challenge or obstacle I am currently facing:

_____

_____

_____

Identifying one action I can take today to overcome this challenge or obstacle, inspired by Dr. Bethune's determination:

_____

_____

Reflect on your day:

5. As you conclude your day, take a moment to reflect on your experiences and progress toward your personal growth and empowerment goals. Consider how Dr. Mary McLeod Bethune's legacy has influenced your actions today and how you can continue to embody her wisdom and lessons in your daily life.

Today's accomplishments and progress:

_____

_____

_____

Areas for growth and improvement:

_____

_____

_____

Goals for tomorrow:

_____

_____

_____

7 Affirmations

1. I am a powerful advocate for justice and equality, following in the footsteps of Dr. Mary McLeod Bethune.

2. My voice matters, and I use it to speak out against injustice and uplift my community.

3. I am inspired by Dr. Bethune's determination and resilience, and I embody these qualities in my own journey.

4. I actively seek opportunities to learn from the wisdom of trailblazing Black women, drawing strength and purpose from their stories.

5. I am an agent of change, using my influence to create a more inclusive and equitable world for future generations.

6. I honor the legacy of Dr. Mary McLeod Bethune by embracing my authentic self and living a life of greatness.

7. I am connected to a powerful sisterhood of Black women, united in our mission to transform the world and empower one another.

CHAPTER 7

TRAILBLAZING TENETS: DEFINING YOUR PATH

Defining Your Path - Daily Worksheet

Date: _____

1. Reflections on Core Commitments:

Key Core Value of Today: _____

How I have aligned my actions with this core value today: _____

2. Purposeful Passion:

My Passion of Focus Today: _____

Action I have taken today to nurture this passion: _____

3. Guiding Grace:

My source of spiritual resilience: _____

Activity done today for cultivating this guiding grace (e.g., meditation, prayer, nature walk, etc.): _____

4. Unyielding Uniqueness:

One unique trait I am celebrating today: _____

How I embraced and demonstrated my authenticity today: _____

5. Trailblazing Action Step:

One step I have taken today on my unique path: _____

End of the Day Reflections:

What I learned about myself today:

_____

_____

_____

End of the Day Reflections:

What I learned about myself today:

_____

_____

_____

How I've become a bit more of a trailblazer today:

_____

_____

_____

One action I plan to take tomorrow to continue defining my path:

_____

_____

_____

Remember, this journey is about progress, not perfection. Each step you take brings you closer to realizing your purpose and the authentic self you are discovering. Be gentle with yourself and celebrate your accomplishments along the way.

7 Affirmations

1. "I embrace the wisdom and strength of trailblazing women like Dr. Mary McLeod Bethune, drawing inspiration from their journeys to guide my own path to greatness."

2. "My core commitments and authentic self serve as my guiding light, empowering me to make a meaningful impact in my life and the lives of others."

3. "I align my actions with my intentions and core values, knowing that this unwavering commitment will propel me towards my personal and professional goals."

4. "With grace and resilience, I overcome challenges and setbacks, trusting that each experience is an opportunity for growth and self-discovery."

5. "I honor the legacy of trailblazing Black women by actively seeking inspiration from their stories, using their experiences to fuel my own journey towards greatness."

6. "By cultivating spiritual resilience and embracing gratitude, I remain grounded and focused on my purpose, even in the face of adversity."

7. "I am a powerful, unique, and authentic individual, and by honoring my true self, I will make a lasting impact on the world around me."

CHAPTER 8

RADIANT RESURGENCE: RECLAIMING YOUR POWER

Daily Empowerment Worksheet

Date: _____

1. Reflect on Your Resilience

Challenge from the past:

_____

_____

_____

How I overcame it:

_____

_____

_____

The strength I developed:

_____

_____

_____

2. Cultivate Self-Love

Self-care activity for today:

_____

_____

_____

Affirmation for the day:

_____

_____

_____

3. Embrace Change

The change I'm currently experiencing:

_____
_____
_____

How can I view this as a growth opportunity?

_____
_____
_____

4. Challenge Limiting Beliefs

Limiting belief that I'm challenging today:

_____
_____
_____

Truth to counteract it:

_____
_____
_____

5. Cultivate a Growth Mindset

The challenge I'm currently facing:

_____
_____

How can I view this as a learning opportunity?

_____
_____
_____

Reflections

What did I learn about myself today?

_____
_____
_____

How am I feeling after today's exercises?

_____
_____
_____

Inspiration from a Black Icon

Today's icon:

_____
_____
_____

Her achievement:

_____
_____
_____

How does her story inspire me?

_____
_____
_____

Remember, this worksheet is a tool for your self-discovery and empowerment journey. Take the time to fill it out with thoughtfulness and honesty. Be kind to yourself throughout the process, and remember that every step you take brings you closer to your authentic self and purpose.

7 Affirmations

1. "I am deeply connected to my roots, drawing strength from the courageous Black women who have come before me."

2. "Every challenge I face is an opportunity for transformation, mirroring the perseverance of **Dr. Mary McLeod Bethune.**"

3. "Just as Dr. Bethune did, I possess the power to change my world and impact my community positively."

4. "Inspired by the legacy of Dr. Bethune, I have the ability to reach my highest potential and achieve greatness."

5. "I am a trailblazer in my own right, paving the way for future generations just as Dr. Bethune did."

6. "In the face of adversity, I am resilient. I rise, just as Dr. Bethune did, rooted in my faith and purpose."

7. "Through self-love and acknowledgment of my worth, I am empowered to create my own legacy, inspired by the life of **Dr. Mary McLeod Bethune.**"

CHAPTER 9

VISIONARY VIBRANCE:
IMAGINING A BRIGHTER FUTURE

The Bethune Blueprint:
Daily Worksheet

Date: _____

Step 1: Dream and Envision

Today, my biggest dream is:

_____
_____
_____

One small thing I can do today to move closer to this dream:

_____
_____
_____

Step 2: Fuel with Hope

A challenge or obstacle I am currently facing:

_____
_____
_____

How I can overcome this obstacle with hope and determination:

_____
_____
_____

Step 3: Plan for Progress

My main goal for today is:

_____
_____

The steps I will take today to achieve this goal are:

i. _____

ii. _____

iii. _____

Step 4: Unlock Your Creative Potential

A new or unconventional idea I have for achieving my goal:

_____

_____

_____

How I can implement this idea today:

_____

_____

_____

Step 5: Take Action

The first action I will take towards my goal today is:

_____

_____

_____

How I feel after taking this action:

_____

_____

_____

Reflections

A lesson I learned from Dr. Mary McLeod Bethune's life today:

_____

_____

_____

How I can apply this lesson to my life:

_____

_____

_____

Affirmation for Today:

I am capable, I am resilient, and I am a creator of my own future. I stand on the shoulders of giants and draw inspiration from their lives. I am following in the footsteps of Dr. Mary McLeod Bethune and many other Black women who have paved the way for me. I will use their stories to fuel my journey toward self-discovery, purpose, and empowerment. Today, I move one step closer to my dreams.

Remember to revisit this worksheet throughout the day, reflecting on your progress and adjusting your plans as needed. This is your journey, and every step, no matter how small, is a step toward your authentic self and purpose.

CHAPTER 10

MASTERING MINDFULNESS: CULTIVATING INNER PEACE

Daily Worksheet

Date: _____

Morning Reflection

Write down your feelings and thoughts as you wake up today:

_____

_____

_____

_____

Cultivate Consciousness

Record three things you notice about your thoughts, feelings, and environment today:

a) _____

b) _____

c) _____

Nurture Introspection

Answer the following self-reflection questions:

a) What am I feeling today?

_____

_____

b) What do I need today?

_____

_____

c) What is my purpose for today?

_____

Find Balance

What activities will you engage in today to maintain balance in the midst of chaos?

a) _____

b) _____

c) _____

Tend to Your Spirit

Choose at least one activity that you will do today to nourish your spirit:

a) Prayer/Meditation

_____

_____

b) Spending time in nature

_____

_____

c) Engaging in a creative pursuit

_____

_____

d) Other

_____

_____

_____

_____

Commit to Healing

What is one step you will take today toward your healing journey?

_____

_____

_____

Evening Reflection

Reflect on your day. Write down any thoughts, feelings, or experiences that stood out:

_____

_____

_____

Remember, each day is a step on your transformative journey. You are powerful, resilient, and capable of great things. Embrace each day with consciousness, introspection, balance, and healing. Honor your spirit and commit to your journey of self-discovery and transformation.

Dr. Mary McLeod Bethune and her son Albert McLeod Bethune, Sr.

7 Affirmations

1. Conscious Clarity: "I am attuned to the world within me and around me; every moment is an opportunity for deeper awareness."

2. Intentional Introspection: "With every introspective thought, I uncover a layer of my true self, weaving together a tapestry of authenticity."

3. Sacred Stillness: "In the midst of life's chaos, I find a sanctuary of peace within, grounding me in serenity and purpose."

4. Harmonious Healing: "Every wound carries the potential for growth. As I tend to my spirit, I embrace healing and transformation."

5. Legacy of Strength: "Guided by the resilience and wisdom of trailblazing women like Dr. Bethune, I forge my path with determination and grace."

6. Unified Purpose: "Bound by a shared history, I draw strength from the stories of those who came before me, and I honor their legacy through my actions."

7. Empowered Self-Reflection: "My reflections are gateways to self-growth. In their depths, I discover the boundless potential that lies within me."

May these affirmations serve as daily reminders and guides on your journey to mastering mindfulness and cultivating inner peace.

Dr. Mary McLeod Bethune with her grandson, Albert McLeod Bethune, Jr., Baby granddaughter, Evelyn Bethune and great grandchildren 1954

CHAPTER 11

BOUNTIFUL BLESSINGS: CULTIVATING GRATITUDE AND GENEROSITY

Daily Worksheet for Transformation and Growth

Date: _____

Morning Reflection:

How am I feeling today?

_____

_____

_____

_____

Daily Affirmation:

Today's Affirmation (example: "I am strong, capable, and ready to make a positive impact.")

Cultivating Gratitude:

Three things I am grateful for today:

1. _____

   _____

2. _____

   _____

3. _____

   _____

Generosity in Action:

One way I can give back to my community today:

_____

_____

_____

Empathy Exercise:

Today, I will seek to understand the experiences or perspectives of:

_____
_____
_____

What I learned from this experience:

_____
_____
_____

Purposeful Philanthropy:

_____
_____
_____

One cause that resonates deeply with me:

_____
_____
_____

How I can support this cause today:

_____
_____
_____

Evening Reflection:

One way my actions have positively impacted others today:

_____
_____
_____

How these actions make me feel:

_____
_____
_____

Inspirational Quote from a Black Icon:

(*example:* "The whole world opened to me when I learned to read."
- Dr. Mary McLeod Bethune)

Today's Quote:

_____
_____
_____

Closing Thought:

_____
_____
_____

One thing I learned about myself today:

_____

_____

_____

Remember, this journey is yours, and each step brings you closer to your authentic self and purpose. Be patient with yourself, and celebrate every small victory along the way.

7 Affirmations

1. "I am inspired by the strength of trailblazers like Dr. Bethune and channel that energy into my own path of purpose."

2. "Every act of kindness I give ripples out into the world, creating a legacy of love and compassion."

3. "I embrace gratitude daily, recognizing the abundance surrounding me and the powerful ancestors guiding me."

4. "Generosity is a reflection of my inner wealth, and I generously share my wisdom and resources to uplift my community."

5. "Empathy is my bridge to deeper connections, understanding, and unity with those around me."

6. "Like Dr. Bethune, I am creating a lasting impact, leaving footsteps for future generations to find their way."

7. "I am on a transformative journey, drawing strength from the stories of Black icons, and I honor that legacy in every step I take."

CHAPTER 12

LEGACY OF LOVE: EMBODYING THE SPIRIT OF DR. MARY MCLEOD BETHUNE

The Bethune Blueprint:
Daily Worksheet

Date: _____

Step 1: Embrace Self-Love

Write one thing you love about yourself today:

_____

_____

_____

Step 2: Educate Yourself

Name one fact you learned about Dr. Mary McLeod Bethune or another Black icon today:

_____

_____

_____

Step 3: Practice Self-Care

List one self-care activity you did today:

_____

_____

_____

Step 4: Engage in Self-Reflection

Reflect on one aspect of your journey to self-discovery and purpose. What progress have you made?

_____

_____

_____

What challenges have you faced?

_____

_____

_____

Step 5: Practice Persistence

List one challenge you faced today and how you overcame it:

_____

_____

_____

Step 6: Cultivate Cultural Appreciation

What aspect of your culture or another culture did you appreciate or learn about today?

_____

_____

_____

Step 7: Embrace Leadership

In what way did you display leadership today?

_____

_____

_____

_____

Step 8: Nurture Inner Strength

Identify one instance today where you drew upon your inner strength:

_____
_____
_____
_____

Affirmation of the Day:

Write down a positive affirmation for yourself based on today's reflections:

_____
_____
_____
_____

Goals for Tomorrow:

What steps will you take tomorrow to continue your journey to self-discovery and greatness?

_____
_____
_____
_____

Remember, you are following in the footsteps of trailblazing Black women. Each day is a new opportunity for growth and transformation. Keep pushing forward, embrace your destiny, and live a life of greatness.

7 Affirmations

1. I am a vessel of transformation, inspired by the legacy of Dr. Mary McLeod Bethune.

2. My journey to self-discovery is guided by the wisdom of trailblazing Black icons who came before me.

3. I embrace challenges as opportunities for growth, just as Dr. Bethune did in her pursuit of greatness.

4. I am a leader in my own right, advocating for justice and effecting positive change within my community.

5. I nurture my inner strength and draw upon it to overcome any obstacle that comes my way.

6. Cultural appreciation is a cornerstone of my journey, fostering unity, understanding, and celebration.

7. I am committed to living a life of purpose, leaving a legacy of love and empowerment for future generations.

TEN REASONS THERE SHOULD BE A MOVIE ABOUT
DR. MARY MCLEOD BETHUNE

1. **Trailblazing Impact:** Dr. Mary McLeod Bethune was a pivotal figure in Black American history. Her story epitomizes determination, resilience, and ambition in the face of adversity, making it an inspiring tale for audiences of all backgrounds.

2. **Highlighting Black Women's Contributions:** Often, historical narratives overlook the significant achievements of Black women. A movie about Dr. Bethune would bring her contributions front and center, filling a noticeable gap in cinematic history.

3. **Educational Value:** Many may not be aware of Dr. Bethune's extensive accomplishments and the breadth of her influence. A movie can serve as an engaging educational tool to introduce her story to a broader audience.

4. **Relevance to Contemporary Issues:** Dr. Bethune's dedication to education, civil rights, and women's rights echoes many of the ongoing battles faced by marginalized groups today. Her story is a testament to the fact that one person can indeed make a difference.

5. **Representation Matters:** For Black audiences, especially Black women, seeing a strong, influential figure like Dr. Bethune on the big screen can be empowering, fostering a sense of pride and belonging.

6. **Historical Context:** Through Dr. Bethune's story, viewers can gain a deeper understanding of the struggles faced by Black Americans in the post-Civil War era, offering a more comprehensive picture of American history.

7. **Intersections of Faith and Activism:** Dr. Bethune's deep faith was integral to her activism. Exploring this dynamic in a film can highlight the complexities and depth of her character, resonating with audiences who share similar convictions.

8. **Champion of Education:** Her commitment to education, particularly for Black girls, in a time when resources and support were minimal, is a remarkable journey that can inspire educators and students alike.

9. **Advisor to Presidents:** Dr. Bethune was not just an educator but also a political activist who advised presidents on child welfare and minority affairs. Her story offers a lens into the inner workings of the highest levels of government.

10. **Legacy and Inspiration:** Beyond her own achievements, Dr. Bethune's story is a beacon of hope and a source of inspiration for anyone facing challenges. A movie about her life serves as a reminder that with passion and perseverance, one can leave a lasting impact on the world.

STAY ENCOURAGED | STAY EMPOWERED | STAY WOKE!

www.ingramcontent.com/pod-product-compliance
Lightning Source LLC
Chambersburg PA
CBHW040003080526
44586CB00027B/2862